STORYWORLD BRIDGES
Teaching Guide

STAGES 10-12

Diana Bentley and Dee Reid

Heinemann

Heinemann is an imprint of Pearson Education Limited, a company incorporated in England and Wales, having its registered office at Edinburgh Gate, Harlow, Essex, CM20 2JE. Registered company number: 872828

Heinemann is a registered trademark of Pearson Education Limitied

© Diana Bentley and Dee Reid, 1999

First published 1999

10
10

Storyworlds Bridges Teaching Guide Stages 10–12 ISBN 9780435143152

This material in this publication is copyright. The photocopy masters may be photocopied for one-time use as instructional material in a classroom, but they may not be copied in unlimited quantities, kept on behalf of others, passed on or sold to third parties, or stored for future use in a retrieval system. If you wish to use the material in any other way than that specified you must apply in writing to the publisher.

Designed and typeset by Artistix, Thame, Oxon.
Photocopy masters illustrated by Cathy Hughes.
Front cover illustrated by Richard Pargeter.
Printed and bound in the UK.

Acknowledgements

We would like to thank the staff and children of the following schools, who trialled *Storyworlds Bridges*:
Butts County Primary School, Alton
Carolside Primary School, Glasgow
Haylands Primary School, Ryde
North Cheshire Jewish Primary School, Cheadle
Rivermead County Primary School, Reading
Sandaig Primary School, Glasgow
St Clements C of E Primary School, Manchester
St Paul's VA Primary School, Chipperfield
Summerbee County First School, Bournemouth
In addition, Locks Heath Junior School assisted Judy Waite in the development of *Star Striker* and *Deep Water*. Thanks also to Chris Moorcroft for her advice on the religious and cultural aspects of *Akbar's Dream*.

CONTENTS

INTRODUCTION

4 THE STORYWORLDS BRIDGES APPROACH
  • Aims • Guided Reading • Guided Writing • Independent work • Assessment
  • Guided Reading Record • Weekly planner

7 HOW DOES STORYWORLDS BRIDGES FIT IN WITH YOUR CURRICULUM?

STAGE 10

8 Teaching Notes: Stage 10
10 Stage 10 PCMs

STAGE 11

14 Teaching Notes: Stage 11
16 Stage 11 PCMs

STAGE 12

20 Teaching Notes: Stage 12
22 Stage 12 PCMs

GENERAL PHOTOCOPY MASTERS

26 General PCMs
30 Assessment PCMs
    Guided Reading Record (inside back cover)

CHART OF COMPONENTS

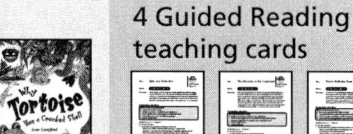

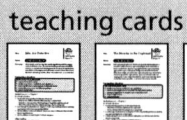

	GUIDED READING	GUIDED READING	GUIDED WRITING
STAGE 10	4 stories	4 Guided Reading teaching cards 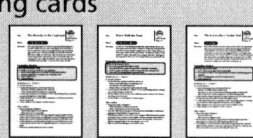	Teaching Guide for Guided Writing and PCMs for Independent Work 
STAGE 11	4 stories	4 Guided Reading teaching cards 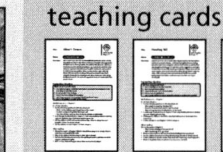 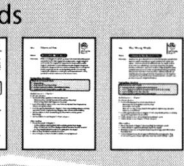	
STAGE 12	4 stories	8 Guided Reading teaching cards 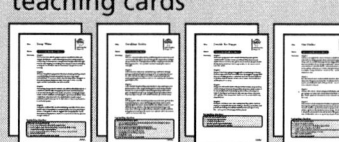	

INTRODUCTION

THE STORYWORLDS BRIDGES APPROACH

AIMS

Storyworlds Bridges is intended for Guided Reading with children in Year 2 (P3) whose progress has been swift, and for those children in Years 3-4 (P4-5) who are ready to move on from a structured reading scheme.

These children have mastered the mechanics of reading and are developing the stamina to tackle longer books. The next stage for these children is to ensure that their comprehension of texts keeps pace with their decoding skills. Storyworlds Bridges provides children with manageable texts for Guided Reading that form a bridge between the controlled language approach of the reading scheme to the demands of reading at National Curriculum Level 3 (Levels B/C in Scotland and Level 3 in Northern Ireland).

Unlike Storyworlds Stages 1-9 (which has a careful introduction of controlled vocabulary), Storyworlds Bridges has no obvious vocabulary control. However, the stories are told in straightforward language that is grammatically easy to read. Repetition of vocabulary and phrases, which is a hallmark of Storyworlds Stages 1-9, is also a feature of Storyworlds Bridges.

The 12 stories meet the range of genres suggested in the National Literacy Strategy for Years 2 and 3 (P3-4) and include:
- stories with familiar settings
- traditional stories
- stories from other cultures
- stories with predictable and patterned language
- extended stories (especially at Stage 12)
- stories by significant children's authors
- different stories by the same author
- texts with language play
- humorous stories

The stories are divided into chapters and give young readers a real sense of reading progress.

GUIDED READING

The National Literacy Strategy *Framework for Teaching* states that the teacher's role in Guided Reading is to support children while they read independently, to help them to use the full range of reading strategies and to assess them for ability grouping. The children are expected to read texts independently and to learn and apply reading strategies.

Guided Reading enables the teacher to assess reading progress by working with a group of children reading at an instructional level (90-95% accuracy). The teacher is able to encourage the children to share their responses and to focus on key aspects of fiction, for example: plot, narrative structures, points of view, setting, character, use of dialogue, themes, genre and language.

GUIDED READING WITH STORYWORLDS BRIDGES

Each Storyworlds Bridges book has its own Guided Reading card, which structures the Guided Reading lesson. Each chapter in the book represents a potential Guided Reading lesson and it is envisaged that the teacher will be able to work with the group for at least one of the chapters. On the cards are suggestions for activities for the teacher and the children to undertake before or after reading each chapter.

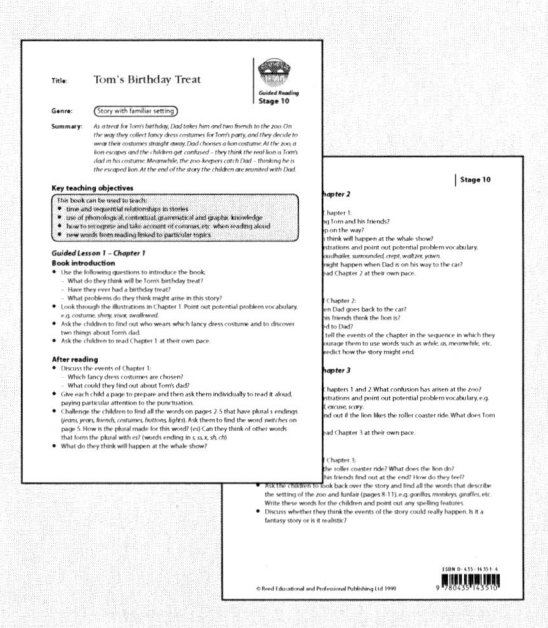

THE STORYWORLDS BRIDGES APPROACH

GUIDED WRITING

The National Literacy Strategy *Framework for Teaching* states that the role of the teacher in Guided Writing is to support children who are writing for themselves, to provide a link between shared and independent writing, to help children who need further reinforcement of basic concepts, to support planning, developing and refining work, and to enable children to evaluate and improve their writing. The child's role is to participate in a supportive group situation, to share and problem-solve aspects of writing with others and to respond positively to other's writing.

Guided Writing forms the parallel activity to Guided Reading. It enables the teacher to work with a group of children to plan, revise and draft their writing. When children plan written work in a group, or bring work in progress to a group, they benefit not only from the guidance of the teacher, but also from the support and advice of their peers.

GUIDED WRITING WITH STORYWORLDS BRIDGES

Each Storyworlds Bridges book has its own suggested activities for before, during, or after Guided Writing sessions. These activities range from planning a story using a story frame to discussing word choices of a piece of writing generated in independent work. Some Guided Writing activities are the springboard for independent writing tasks; some independent work becomes the subject of the Guided Writing session. These linked activities are clearly indicated in the Teaching Guide.

INDEPENDENT WORK

Some independent sessions will obviously be used for the group to undertake the reading of specific chapters. For other sessions the Teaching Guide provides a range of activities for the group to undertake, including a photocopy master (PCM) for each book. These could be completed independently and then discussed in a Guided Writing session or in a plenary session.

A set of four general PCMs is provided to help structure children's writing and response to stories. Suggestions for the use of these PCMs has been provided in the teaching notes for each title. However, these PCMs could also be used with any book at the teacher's discretion.

ASSESSMENT

The assessment PCM at Stage 10 (page 30) mirrors the kind of questions that children meet in the Level 2 Reading Comprehension paper in SATs at the end of Key Stage 1 (and similar national tests in Scotland and Northern Ireland). The assessment PCMs for Stages 11 and 12 (pages 31 and 32) are similar to the questions posed in the Level 3 (extension) paper.

To achieve a high mark, the children not only have to read with accuracy but they also have to be able to infer meaning and to support any response they make with reference to the text. Many able readers often recognise the obvious answer and rush to write this down. However, to achieve good marks they need to read carefully and extract all the relevant information.

GUIDED READING RECORD

The PCM inside the back cover is a Guided Reading assessment record sheet. It enables the teacher to track the progress of individual children and groups during the Guided Reading session.

THE STORYWORLDS BRIDGES APPROACH

WEEKLY PLANNER

The weekly plans below show how work with *Storyworlds 4–9* and *Storyworlds Bridges* could be planned over a two-week period to cover Guided Reading and Guided Writing. These plans could be used as models and adapted as necessary, depending on the needs and abilities of your class.

WEEK 1 — GUIDED READING

	A (most able)	B (able)	C (average)	D (average)	E (weak)
MON	**Guided Reading** *Akbar's Dream* Chapter 1 (Bridges 11)	Pre-reading *Monster in the Cupboard* Ch.1 (Bridges 10)	Listen to a story tape	Storyworlds PCM Phonic practice	OA Practice reading Storyworlds 4–6
TUES	Independent reading *Akbar's Dream* Chapter 2	**Guided Reading** *Monster in the Cupboard* Chapter 2	Pre-reading Storyworlds 7–9	OA Practice reading Storyworlds 7–9	Storyworlds workbook
WED	Word level work based on shared lesson	Word level work based on shared lesson	**Guided Reading** Storyworlds 7–9	Word level work based on shared lesson	Word level work based on shared lesson
THUR	Text level work based on shared lesson	Text level work based shared lesson	Text level work based on shared lesson	**Guided Reading** Storyworlds 7–9	Text level work based on shared lesson
FRI	PCM Speech bubbles (p16)	PCM Finish the sentences (p12)	Storyworlds Workbook	Storyworlds Workbook	**Guided Reading** Storyworlds 4–6

WEEK 2 — GUIDED WRITING

	A (most able)	B (able)	C (average)	D (average)	E (weak)
MON	Independent writing describing the Taj Mahal	Pre-writing General PCM: Character study (p28)	Pre-writing Storyworlds 7–9	OA Pre-writing Storyworlds 7–9	**Guided Writing**
TUES	**Guided Writing**	Bridges: Guided Reading word level activity	Storyworlds Workbook	Storyworlds Workbook 7–9	OA Phonic/spelling games
WED	Word level work based on shared lesson	**Guided Writing**	Word level work based on shared lesson	Word level work based on shared lesson	Word level work based on shared lesson
THUR	Text level work based on shared lesson	Text level work based on shared lesson	**Guided Writing**	Text level work based on shared lesson	Text level work based on shared lesson
FRI	Independent reading *Akbar's Dream* Chapter 3	Independent reading *Monster in the Cupboard* Chapter 3	Independent reading Storyworlds 7–9	**Guided Writing**	Listen to a story tape

HOW DOES STORYWORLDS BRIDGES FIT IN WITH YOUR CURRICULUM?

NATIONAL CURRICULUM/NATIONAL LITERACY STRATEGY ENGLAND AND WALES

Storyworlds Bridges is specifically designed to meet the requirements of the National Curriculum in England and Wales (for children working within level 3), and the detailed guidance for meeting these statutory requirements provided in the *Framework for Teaching* of the National Literacy Strategy.

- **Speaking and listening:** the stories are ideal for developing skills of speaking, listening, group discussion and interaction during Guided Reading sessions.
- **Reading:** all of the reading skills identified in the National Curriculum are catered for in the challenging and stimulating stories.
- **Writing:** ample opportunity is offered for modelled writing and developing a range of writing skills.
- **Range of text types:** as described on page 4, the 12 stories in Storyworlds Bridges meet the range of fiction genres suggested in the NLS for Years 2 and 3.
- **Coverage of objectives:** each of the stories can be used to teach specific objectives described in the *Framework for Teaching* at text, sentence and word level. Each PCM in this book identifies objectives as follows: year and term (e.g. Y2T2), level and objective number (e.g. S6/7 – sentence level 6 and 7).

ENGLISH IN THE NORTHERN IRELAND CURRICULUM

Storyworlds Bridges can be used to deliver key elements of the DENI Programme of Study for English, for children working within level 3.

- **Talking and listening:** children should be encouraged to participate in a wide range of talking and listening activities arising from their work on the stories. In particular, the stories could be used to develop a sense of context, audience and purpose for such activities.
- **Reading:** the 12 stories provide a rich range of opportunities for reading activities in which children could develop their abilities of reading, understanding and engaging with texts. They should be given opportunities to read in a range of contexts, and for a range of purposes and audiences.
- **Writing:** a range of writing opportunities could be drawn from the children's experience of reading the stories, which should provide a variety of purposes, contexts and audiences. Children should have opportunities to write in a variety of forms and to plan their work in a range of different ways.

ENGLISH LANGUAGE 5-14 (SCOTTISH NATIONAL GUIDELINES)

Storyworlds Bridges is suitable for delivering the requirements of the English Language 5–14 guidelines in Scotland, for children working at levels B–C.

- **Listening/watching:** the stories provide opportunities for children to develop their skills of listening in groups, listening in order to respond to texts, awareness of genre, and knowledge about language.
- **Talking:** children should be encouraged to discuss the stories in groups, and talk about their feelings, experiences and opinions in relation to the stories. Their response to the stories should be developed alongside their awareness of audience.
- **Reading:** the stimulating stories in Storyworlds Bridges provide many opportunities for reading for enjoyment, plus reflecting on the writer's ideas and craft. The stories also provide opportunities to develop awareness of a range of text types (see page 4) and knowledge about language.
- **Writing:** opportunities to engage in a range of writing (e.g. personal, imaginative) are provided by the stories, as well as developing skills of structuring, punctuation, spelling, handwriting and presentation.

STAGE 10

Notes on guided reading are contained on the *Guided Reading card* for each book.

BOOK	NLS FIT	GUIDED WRITING
 *Jake Ace Detective*	Year 2 Term 1	**TEXT LEVEL WORK** • Using the story frame (general PCM, page 29), help the group to sort out the story into problems and solutions. Encourage them to see the links between the two. Write their suggestions on to the frame. **SENTENCE LEVEL WORK/WORD LEVEL WORK** • Using the writing produced in independent work ('The day I found a kitten') discuss ways of improving their writing by looking at its structure, choice of language and spelling. Encourage peer group responses.
 *Tom's Birthday Treat*	Year 2 Term 1	**TEXT LEVEL WORK** • Look back at pages 18–20 of the story. Ask the group to imagine that they are reporters visiting the zoo. Ask them to make notes about the things they saw and heard as the children persuaded 'Dad' to get into the waltzer. Discuss the purpose of the reporter's notes and the intended audience. Show them the general PCM (page 27) for completion in independent work. **SENTENCE LEVEL WORK** • Talk to the group about the differences between direct and reported speech. Look at pages 18–20 of the story. Ask the children to change some of the direct speech into reported speech. Discuss the language changes they have to make.
 *The Monster in the Cupboard*	Year 2 Term 1	**WORD LEVEL WORK** • Write the verbs *run – running* and *bump – bumping*. What do the children notice happens when *ing* is added? Look through Chapter 1 and find other examples of verbs ending with *ing*, e.g. *trying, standing*. Can the group devise a rule to explain what happens when *ing* is added? Make a chart for each 'rule'. Ask the group where they would put the following words: *sit, scare, go, live, cry, grin*. **TEXT LEVEL WORK** • Using writing produced in independent work (character study), extend the children's use of descriptive language.
 *Why Tortoise Has a Cracked Shell*	Year 2 Term 2	**TEXT LEVEL WORK** • Ask the group to bring their completed Assessment PCM (page 30). Discuss the answers and guide their written responses to be as full as possible. **SENTENCE LEVEL WORK** • Ask the group to look through chapter 1 of the story to find verbs in the past tense ending with *ed*, e.g. *watched, called, slithered*. Point out verbs that change in the past tense, e.g. *met, sat, had*. Make a chart of all the verbs showing the present and past tense forms.

INDEPENDENT WORK

TEXT LEVEL WORK
- Ask the group to list all of Jake's solutions to the problems in the story (what he did with each kitten and how he worked out the mystery owner).

- Ask the group to write independently, using the writing prompt: 'The day I found a kitten...'. They should bring this work to the Guided Writing session.

WORD LEVEL WORK
- Give the group the PCM: adding capital letters (page 10).

WORD LEVEL WORK
- Look at pages 2–7 of the story and collect all the words that contain 'ea'. Ask the children to investigate the range of sounds made by the vowel phoneme, and then to list the words according to their sounds:
  - *jeans*: ear, treat, screamed, please, sea
  - *early*: earthlings, heard
  - *wear*: wearing
  - *breakfast*
  - *great*
  - *years*

  Which sound has the greatest number of words?

TEXT LEVEL WORK
- Ask the group to complete the general PCM: Reporter's notebook (page 27), describing the events on pages 18–20 of the story, where 'Dad' is persuaded to get into the waltzer.

- Give the group the PCM: sequencing the story (page 11).

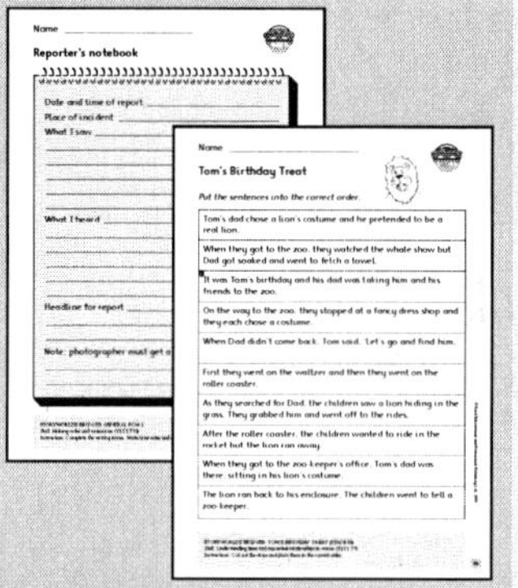

TEXT LEVEL WORK
- Complete the general PCM: Character study (page 28). (They should bring this work to the Guided Writing session.)

- Give the group the PCM: reasons for events (page 12).

WORD LEVEL WORK
- Ask the group to make a collection of words linked to the school setting of the story e.g. *term, school, playtime*, etc.

TEXT LEVEL WORK
- Complete the general PCM: Assessment (page 30). They should bring this work to the Guided Writing session.

WORD LEVEL WORK
- Give the group the following words and ask them to write a short definition of the word: *hopped, slithered, purred, hunched, prowled*. When they have written their definitions they should compare their answers.

- Give the group the PCM: completing the chart (page 13).

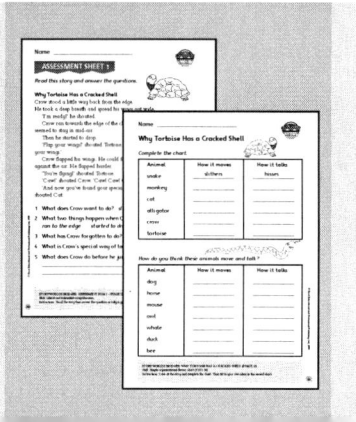

Jake, Ace Detective

Look at the reasons for the capital letters.

Title → **Not Another Kitten**

Starting a sentence → The next day, I went to the surgery with Mum. Sitting on the doorstep was another cardboard box.

Person's name → 'Oh no!' I said. 'I do hope this isn't another of Mrs Price's kittens.'

The pronoun 'I' → I picked up the box. It felt very light. I opened the box and looked inside. There wasn't a kitten – there were six white mice!

Now add the capital letters to the rest of the story.

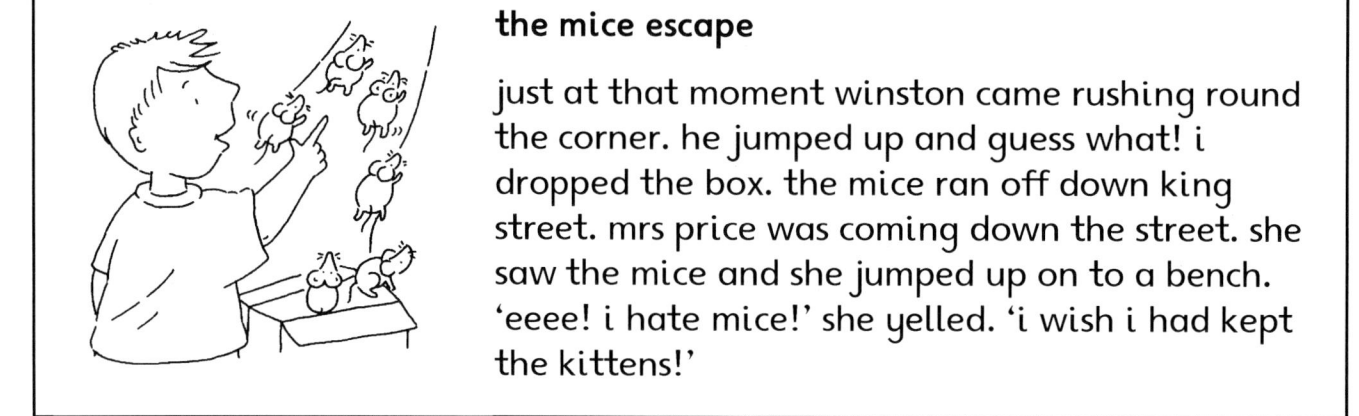

the mice escape

just at that moment winston came rushing round the corner. he jumped up and guess what! i dropped the box. the mice ran off down king street. mrs price was coming down the street. she saw the mice and she jumped up on to a bench. 'eeee! i hate mice!' she yelled. 'i wish i had kept the kittens!'

STORYWORLDS BRIDGES: JAKE, ACE DETECTIVE (STAGE 10)
Skill: Using capital letters (Y2T1 S5).
Instructions: Look at the reason for capital letters. Write out the text, using capitals correctly.

Name _____

Tom's Birthday Treat

Put the sentences into the correct order.

Tom's dad chose a lion's costume and he pretended to be a real lion.

When they got to the zoo, they watched the whale show but Dad got soaked and went to fetch a towel.

①It was Tom's birthday and his dad was taking him and his friends to the zoo.

On the way to the zoo, they stopped at a fancy dress shop and they each chose a costume.

When Dad didn't come back, Tom said, 'Let's go and find him.'

First they went on the waltzer and then they went on the roller coaster.

As they searched for Dad, the children saw a lion hiding in the grass. They grabbed him and went off to the rides.

After the roller coaster, the children wanted to ride in the rocket but the lion ran away.

When they got to the zoo-keeper's office, Tom's dad was there, sitting in his lion's costume.

The lion ran back to his enclosure. The children went to tell a zoo-keeper.

STORYWORLDS BRIDGES: TOM'S BIRTHDAY TREAT (STAGE 10)
Skill: Understanding time and sequential relationships in stories (Y2T1 T4).
Instructions: Cut out the strips and place them in the correct order.

The Monster in the Cupboard

Finish the sentences. The words in the box will help you.

| scared   monster   cupboard   bully   Mr Bailey |
| playground   scratching   thumping   noise   teacher |

Emily and her friend, Rosie, did not like Kevin Brown because __
_____

Kevin teased the new children by telling them that _____
_____

Kevin went into the empty classroom with Emily because _____
_____

When they got near the cupboard, Emily and Kevin could hear __
_____

Kevin rushed out of the classroom because _____
_____

Emily did not rush away because she knew that _____
_____

Name _____

Why Tortoise Has a Cracked Shell

Complete the chart.

Animal	How it moves	How it talks
snake	slithers	hisses
monkey		
cat		
alligator		
crow		
tortoise		

How do you think these animals move and talk?

Animal	How it moves	How it talks
dog		
horse		
mouse		
owl		
whale		
duck		
bee		

STORYWORLDS BRIDGES: WHY TORTOISE HAS A CRACKED SHELL (STAGE 10)
Skill: Simple organisational device: chart (Y2T1 S6).
Instructions: Look at the story and complete the chart. Then fill in your own ideas in the second chart.

STAGE 11

Notes on guided reading are contained on the *Guided Reading card* for each book.

BOOK	NLS FIT	GUIDED WRITING

Akbar's Dream

Year 2 Term 2

TEXT LEVEL WORK
- Using the story frame (general PCM, page 29), help the group to sort out the story into problems and solutions. Encourage them to see the links between the two, e.g. *problem* – very expensive to visit the Taj Mahal; *solution* – Grandfather's savings and the sale of Akbar's cloth.

SENTENCE LEVEL WORK/WORD LEVEL WORK
- Using the writing produced in independent work ('A description of the Taj Mahal'), discuss ways of improving writing by looking at its structure, choice of language and spelling. Encourage peer group responses.

The Wrong Words

Year 2 Term 3

TEXT LEVEL WORK
- Look at the jokes that Merry and Daryl tell each other in the story and discuss the way these jokes have been presented. Ask the children if they know any jokes and decide how their jokes should be written down.

WORD LEVEL WORK
- Remind the group that in the story Merry makes up words to rhyme with *Daryl*. Ask the group to think of rhyming words to go with their names. Discuss how these would be spelled, using their phonological knowledge. They should try to think of different ways of presenting the rhyming sound, e.g. Dar*yl*, barr*el*, Car*ol*.

Standing Tall

Year 2 Term 1

TEXT LEVEL WORK
- Give each member of the group a copy of the general PCM: Book review (page 26) and help them to complete it. Ensure that they make reference to the episodes in the text to support their judgements.

WORD LEVEL WORK
- Ask each member of the group to take it in turn to suggest a word that starts with a single consonant. They should all write down these words. Then ask them to each suggest a word starting with a double consonant and finally ask them to suggest a word beginning with a triple consonant. Discuss any spelling errors and ask them to explore how they might learn how to spell any difficult words.

Storm at Sea

Year 2 Term 1

TEXT LEVEL WORK
- Ask the group to bring their completed Assessment PCM (page 31). Discuss the answers and guide their written responses to be as full as possible.

- Using the story frame (general PCM, page 29), help the group to sort out the story into problems and solutions. Encourage them to see links between the two. Write their suggestions on to the frame.

INDEPENDENT WORK

TEXT LEVEL WORK
- Ask the group to look at the description and the illustrations of the Taj Mahal on pages 22–27 of the story. Ask them to write two paragraphs; one describing the outside and the other the inside of the Taj Mahal. They should imagine that they are Akbar, telling his Uncle Omar about the beautiful building. They should bring this work to the Guided Writing session.

SENTENCE LEVEL WORK
- Give group the PCM: changing reported speech into direct speech (page 16).

TEXT LEVEL WORK
- Give the group a copy of the general PCM: Reporter's notebook (page 27). Ask them to complete the frame, imagining that they are the policeman who went to Uncle Max's house.

- Ask the children to write down three jokes each for the class to read. Remind them how to present the jokes so that the reader knows who is speaking.

SENTENCE LEVEL WORK/WORD LEVEL WORK
- Give the group the PCM: correcting sentences (page 17).

WORD LEVEL WORK
- Ask the children to look through Chapter 3 of the story and to find 10 different compound words.

TEXT LEVEL WORK
- Ask the children to list all the things that tell the reader that Carrie is not happy in her new school: e.g. she feels shy; she has few friends; no-one seems to notice her; Mandy makes fun of her; she is unhappy when she gets home, etc.

- Give the group PCM: describing characters (page 18).

WORD LEVEL WORK
- Ask the group to make a collection of words from the story that describe how the characters speak, e.g. *asked, shouted, yelled, whined.*

TEXT LEVEL WORK
- Complete the general PCM: Assessment (page 31). They should bring this work to the Guided Writing session.

- Give the group the PCM: story setting (page 19).

- Ask the group to complete the general PCM: Book review (page 26).

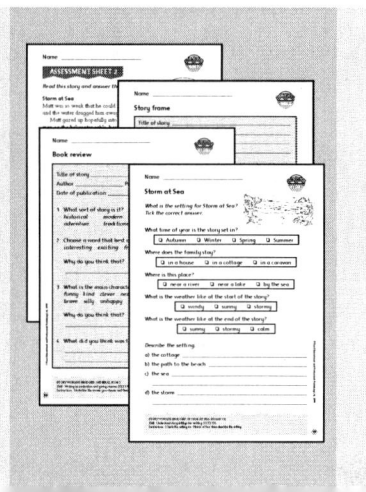

Akbar's Dream

Write in the speech bubbles, the words spoken by each character.

Akbar said that he wanted to make the most beautiful silk pattern.

I want to _____

Grandfather said that they must go to see the Taj Mahal.

Uncle Omar said he would buy Akbar's silk.

Akbar said that he wanted to make a pattern with the flowers and the leaves.

STORYWORLDS BRIDGES: AKBAR'S DREAM (STAGE 11)
Skill: Ways of presenting speech; speech bubbles (Y2T2 S6/7).
Instructions: Change reported speech to direct speech, using speech bubbles.

Name _____

The Wrong Words

What does Merry mean to say?
Write out the words in the correct order.

I to a want for go walk.

_____

What for we having are tea?

_____

Do know good any you jokes?

_____

You best friend my are Daryl.

_____

Sometimes get I words my muddled.

_____

Sometimes Merry muddles the words.
Write out the sentences correctly.

I like to eat chish and fips.

_____

I like jelling tokes.

_____

I beed a new nattery.

_____

I lan cay sots of rhymes.

_____

A mobot can rake you laugh.

_____

STORYWORLDS BRIDGES: THE WRONG WORDS (STAGE 11)
Skill: Exploring humorous writing (Y2T3 T6).
Instructions: Write out the sentences correctly.

Name _____

Standing Tall

*Underline the word that you think best describes each character.
Then find evidence in the story to support your view.*

I think Carrie is (brave   shy   noisy   kind) when she

_____

_____

I think Mandy is (greedy   nasty   cruel   silly) when she

_____

_____

I think Mum is (patient   kind   thoughtful   foolish) when she

_____

_____

I think Miss Wallace is (sad   generous   patient   cross) when she

_____

_____

I think Ben is (selfish   scared   happy   impatient) when he

_____

_____

STORYWORLDS BRIDGES: STANDING TALL (STAGE 11)
Skill: Describing characters, expressing own views and using words and phrases from the text (Y2T2 T6).
Instruction: Underline the characteristic and then find words or phrases from the text that support your view.

Name _____

Storm at Sea

What is the setting for Storm at Sea?
Tick the correct answer.

What time of year is the story set in?

❏ Autumn   ❏ Winter   ❏ Spring   ❏ Summer

Where does the family stay?

❏ in a house   ❏ in a cottage   ❏ in a caravan

Where is this place?

❏ near a river   ❏ near a lake   ❏ by the sea

What is the weather like at the start of the story?

❏ windy   ❏ sunny   ❏ stormy

What is the weather like at the end of the story?

❏ sunny   ❏ stormy   ❏ calm

Describe the setting.

a) the cottage _____

b) the path to the beach _____

c) the sea _____

_____

d) the storm _____

_____

STORYWORLDS BRIDGES: STORM AT SEA (STAGE 11)
Skill: Understand story settings for writing (Y2T2 S5).
Instructions: Check the setting for 'Storm at Sea' then describe the setting.

STAGE 12

Notes on guided reading are contained on the Guided Reading card for each book.

BOOK	NLS FIT	GUIDED WRITING
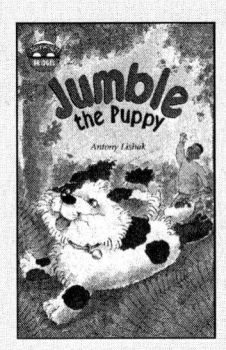 Jumble the Puppy	Year 2 Term 3	**TEXT LEVEL WORK** • Using the story frame (general PCM, page 29), help the group to sort out the story into problems and solutions. Encourage them to see links between the two. Write their suggestions on to the story frame. **SENTENCE LEVEL WORK/WORD LEVEL WORK** • Using the writing produced in independent work ('Gold at last'), discuss ways of improving writing by looking at its structure, choice of language and spelling. Encourage peer group responses.
 Star Striker	Year 2 Term 3	**TEXT LEVEL WORK** • Give the group a copy of the general PCM: Reporter's notebook (page 27). Cut out a report of a football match from a newspaper and discuss how to write the report of an exciting match. Ask them to imagine what it must have been like in Sasha's grandfather's time, when he scored the winning goal. Show them how to make notes about what they saw and what they heard from the crowd. **SENTENCE LEVEL WORK** • Ask the group to bring their completed PCM (page 23). Discuss their answers and check that all the children can spell *who, what, where, when, why, how* from memory.
 Deep Water	Year 2 Term 3	**WORD LEVEL WORK** • Talk about synonyms and other alternative words and phrases that express same or similar meanings. Ask if they can remember any of the descriptions that Jenny uses to describe her feelings. Ask how they feel when they are nervous and encourage them to write down their suggestions. Finally, see how many synonyms they can suggest for *scared*. **TEXT LEVEL WORK** • Ask the group to bring their completed general PCM: Book review (page 26) and discuss their answers with them. Explain to the children how they need to extract evidence from the text to support their judgements.
 Greyfriars Bobby	Year 2 Term 3	**TEXT LEVEL WORK** • Discuss how they recognise that this is a 'true' story, as opposed to a fictional story. Ask them to select evidence from Chapter 1 of the story. Write down their suggestions and show them how to present the evidence in the form of bullet points. Ask them to look through Chapter 2 of the story and do the same. Help them to present their evidence succinctly, e.g. *events connected to history*. • Ask the group to bring their completed Assessment PCM (page 32). Discuss the answers and guide their written responses to be as full as possible.

INDEPENDENT WORK

TEXT LEVEL WORK
- Ask the group to list all the arguments that Dan gives to his parents to persuade them to let him have a dog. Then ask the group to make a parallel list of all the naughty things that Jumble does.

- Ask the group to write two paragraphs imagining how Dan and Jumble find a hoard of pirates' gold in Smugglers Wood. They should title the work *Finding the Pirates' Gold*. They should bring this work to the Guided Writing session.

WORD LEVEL WORK
- Give the group the PCM: finding synonyms for 'said' (page 22).

TEXT LEVEL WORK
- Give each child a copy of the general PCM: Character study (page 28).

WORD LEVEL WORK
- Ask the children to look through Chapter 1 of the story and to list all the words ending with *ly*. They should write out each word as it is in the story and then split the word into *the root word + ly*, e.g. *real + ly = really*.

SENTENCE LEVEL WORK
- Give the group the PCM: forming questions (page 23).

TEXT LEVEL WORK
- Ask the group to complete the general PCM: 'Book review' (page 26). They should bring this work to the Guided Writing session.

WORD LEVEL WORK
- Ask the children to look through Chapter 1 of the story and to make a list of all the words starting with *th*. They should then look at the word, cover it with a ruler and see if they can write it correctly from memory: *thought, they, that, think, them, they're, this, through, that*.

SENTENCE LEVEL WORK
- Give the group the PCM: recognising verb tenses (page 24).

TEXT LEVEL WORK
- Complete the general PCM: Assessment (page 32). They should bring this work to the Guided Writing session.

- Ask the children to skim through the story and to make a list of all the things that Bobby does that show his devotion to Old Jock. Remind the children about the tricks he does for Old Jock, as well as the way he protects him.

WORD LEVEL WORK
- Give the group the PCM: vocabulary (page 25).

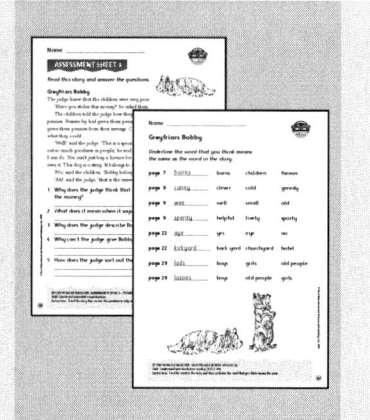

STAGE 12

Name _____

Jumble the Puppy

Look through pages 3–23 of the story.
Find 10 different ways that describe people speaking.

page 1 ___said Tom___   page _____

page _____   page _____

page _____   page _____

page _____   page _____

page _____   page _____

Use the words you have found to fill in the gaps below.

'Dogs need looking after,' _____said_____ Mum.

'Please let me have a puppy!' _____ Tom.

'Where is Jumble?' _____ Mum.

'I'll make sure he behaves,' _____ Tom.

'Perhaps he could stay in a kennel,' _____ Dad.

'Help, help! I'm over here!' _____ Dad.

STORYWORLDS BRIDGES: JUMBLE THE PUPPY (STAGE 12)
Skill: Recognising alternative words for tagged speech (Y2T3 W10).
Instructions: Read through pages 3–23 to find alternative words for tagged speech, then use them to complete the sentences.

Name _____

Star Striker

Write the question to go with each answer. The words in the box will help you.

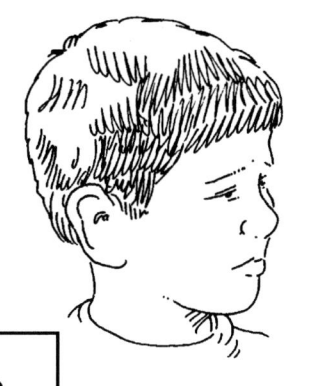

| who   what   when   why   where |

Question: _____
Answer: Sasha was unhappy because she had no friends.

Question: _____
Answer: At playtime Sasha sat alone on a wooden bench.

Question: _____
Answer: Ben liked to eat Super Chew bubble gum.

Question: _____
Answer: Ben went to Sasha's house after school.

Question: _____
Answer: Mum made toffee pie for tea.

Question: _____
Answer: Dad found the photograph of Grandad in the cabinet.

Question: _____
Answer: Derry Dazzle was Grandad.

STORYWORLDS BRIDGES: STAR STRIKER (STAGE 12)
Skill: Turning statements into questions (Y2T3 S6).
Instructions: Read the answers and then write the questions to go with them.

Name _____

Deep Water

Decide if each verb is in the present or past tense. Tick the chart.

	past	present
Miss Walker **asked** the class to prepare a speech.		
Jenny **hated** reading aloud to the class.		
Mum said, 'You **grow** too quickly.'		
Jenny **picked** up Lee's watch.		
'She **has** my watch!' shouted Lee.		
'**Give** Lee his watch and then see the Headmaster.'		
'I **wanted** to wear it while I was doing my speech,' said Jenny.		
Mr Atkins said, 'What **is** it you want to say?'		

Correct the sentences below.

Yesterday the class ask her lots of questions.
_____

'You can borrow my watch, if you liked,' said Lee.
_____

'I swim this morning before school,' said Jenny.
_____

STORYWORLDS BRIDGES: DEEP WATER (STAGE 12)
Skill: Recognising the past or present tense (Y2T2 S5).
Instructions: Tick the correct form of the verb and then correct the sentences.

Greyfriars Bobby

Underline the word that you think means the same as the word in the story.

page 7	<u>bairns</u>	barns	children	farmer
page 9	<u>canny</u>	clever	cold	greedy
page 9	<u>wee</u>	well	small	old
page 9	<u>sperity</u>	helpful	lively	sporty
page 22	<u>aye</u>	yes	eye	no
page 22	<u>kirkyard</u>	back yard	churchyard	hotel
page 29	<u>lads</u>	boys	girls	old people
page 29	<u>lassies</u>	boys	old people	girls

STORYWORLDS BRIDGES: GREYFRIARS BOBBY (STAGE 12)
Skill: Understand new words from reading (Y2T3 W9).
Instructions: Find the word in the story and then underline the word that you think means the same.

Name _____

Book review

Title of story _____

Author _____ Publisher _____

Date of publication _____

1 What sort of story is it?
   historical   modern   travel   school
   adventure   traditional   true   fantasy

2 Choose a word that best describes the story.
   interesting exciting frightening sad realistic dull

   Why do you think that?
   _____

3 What is the main character like?
   funny kind clever nervous selfish foolish mean
   brave silly unhappy thoughtful happy jolly

   Why do you think that?
   _____

4 What did you think was the best part of the story?
   _____
   _____

STORYWORLDS BRIDGES: GENERAL PCM 1
Skill: Writing an evaluation and giving reasons (Y2T3 T12).
Instructions: Underline the answer you choose and then say why you chose it.

Name _____

Reporter's notebook

Date and time of report _____

Place of incident _____

What I saw _____
_____
_____
_____
_____
_____

What I heard _____
_____
_____
_____
_____

Headline for report _____
_____
_____

Note: photographer must get a photograph of _____
_____
_____

STORYWORLDS BRIDGES: GENERAL PCM 2
Skill: Making notes and summaries (Y2T3 T19).
Instruction: Complete the writing frame. Write brief notes and comments.

Name _____

Character study

Title of book _____
Author _____
Name of character _____
_____
_____

Circle four words that describe your chosen character.

clever   proud   nervous   silly   generous
dreamy   kind   funny   polite   mean
untruthful   happy   sporty   friendly

Find evidence in the text to support your view.

1 I think _____ is _____ when
   _____

2 I also think that _____
   _____
   _____

3 Finally, I think _____
   _____
   _____
   _____

STORYWORLDS BRIDGES: GENERAL PCM 3
Skill: Using evidence for character analysis (Y2T2 T14).
Instruction: Complete the writing frame. Write brief notes and comments.

Name _____

Story frame

Title of story _____

Author _____ Illustrator _____

Characters _____

Setting _____

Problems	Solutions

How is the main problem finally solved?

STORYWORLDS BRIDGES: GENERAL PCM 4
Skill: Identifying problems and solutions from texts (Y2T3 general).
Instruction: Complete the writing frame. Write brief notes and comments.

Name _____

ASSESSMENT SHEET 1

Read this story and answer the questions.

Why Tortoise Has a Cracked Shell

Crow stood a little way back from the edge.
He took a deep breath and spread his wings out wide.
   'I'm ready!' he shouted.
   Crow ran towards the edge of the cliff. For a moment, he seemed to stay in mid-air.
   Then he started to drop.
   'Flap your wings!' shouted Tortoise. 'You've forgotten to flap your wings.'
   Crow flapped his wings. He could feel his feathers pushing against the air. He flapped harder.
   'You're flying!' shouted Tortoise.
   'Caw!' shouted Crow. 'Caw! Caw! Caw! This is wonderful!'
   'And now you've found your special way of talking too,' shouted Cat.

1 What does Crow want to do?   *slither   swing   swim   fly*   1 mark

2 What two things happen when Crow jumps off the edge?
   ran to the edge   started to drop   stayed in mid-air   2 marks

3 What has Crow forgotten to do? _____   2 marks

4 What is Crow's special way of talking? _____   2 marks

5 What does Crow do before he jumps off the edge?
   _____
   _____   5 marks

Total: ☐

STORYWORLDS BRIDGES: ASSESSMENT PCM 1 – STAGE 10
Skill: Literal and inferential comprehension.
Instructions: Read the story then answer the questions as fully as you can.

Name _____

ASSESSMENT SHEET 2

Read this story and answer the questions.

Storm at Sea

Matt was so weak that he could hardly swim and the water dragged him away from the ledge.

Matt gazed up hopefully into the sky. He saw the man on the helicopter cable, hovering above him.

'Don't worry, son! I'll have you out of the sea in no time!' he called to Matt. The next moment, Matt felt the man's strong arms putting him into the safety of the harness. 'Having a quick swim, were you?' joked the man.

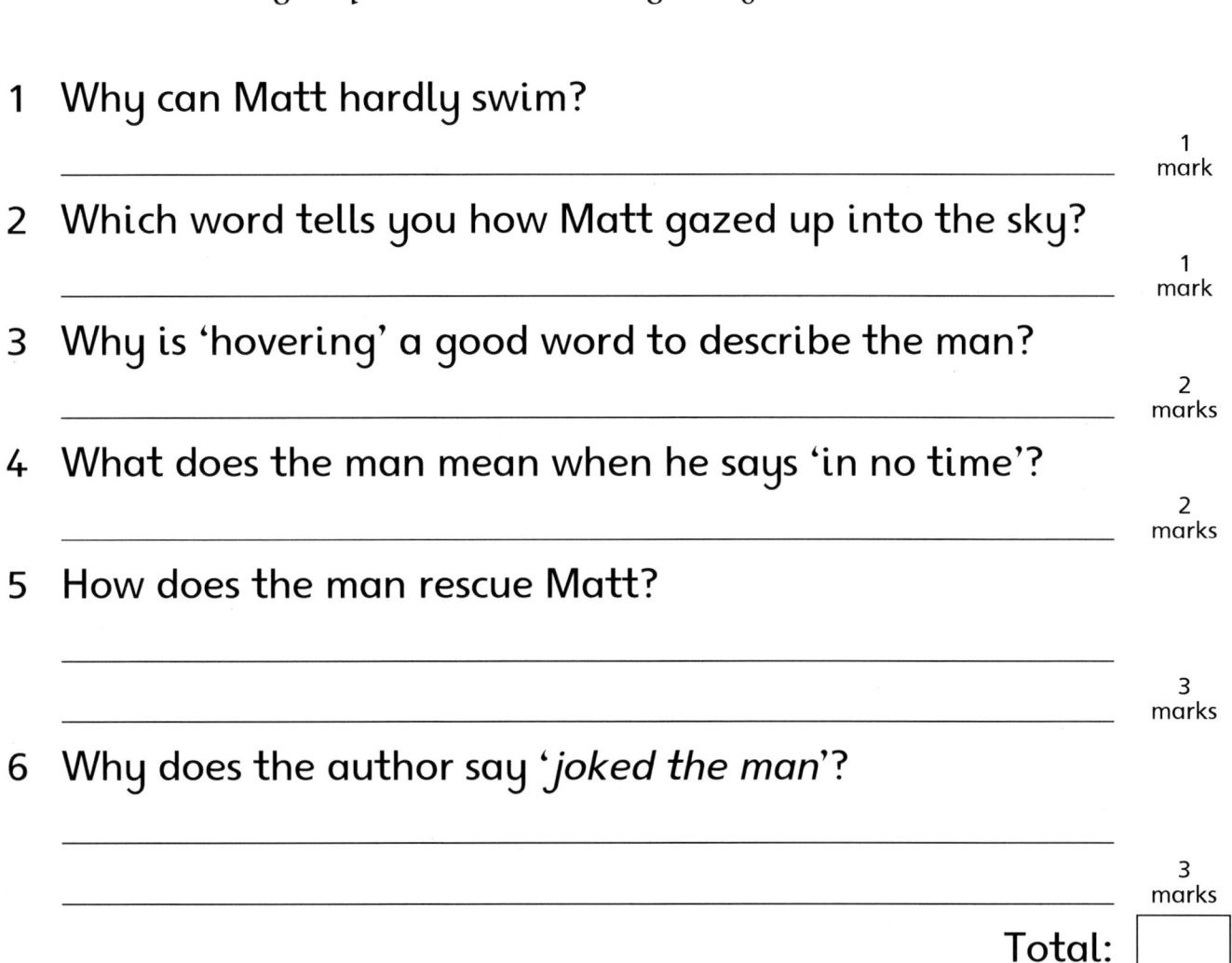

1 Why can Matt hardly swim?

_____
1 mark

2 Which word tells you how Matt gazed up into the sky?

_____
1 mark

3 Why is 'hovering' a good word to describe the man?

_____
2 marks

4 What does the man mean when he says 'in no time'?

_____
2 marks

5 How does the man rescue Matt?

_____
_____
3 marks

6 Why does the author say '*joked the man*'?

_____
_____
3 marks

Total: [ ]

STORYWORLDS BRIDGES: ASSESSMENT PCM 2 – STAGE 11
Skill: Literal and inferential comprehension.
Instructions: Read the story then answer the questions as fully as you can.

Name _____

ASSESSMENT SHEET 3

Read this story and answer the questions.

Greyfriars Bobby

The judge knew that the children were very poor.

'Have you stolen this money?' he asked them.

The children told the judge how they had all collected the pennies. Passers-by had given them pennies. Old people had given them pennies from their savings. Children had given what they could.

'Well!' said the judge. 'This is a special dog that can bring out so much goodness in people,' he said. 'But there is nothing I can do. You can't just buy a licence for any dog. You have to own it. This dog is a stray. It belongs to nobody.'

'No,' said the children. 'Bobby belongs to everybody.'

'Ah!' said the judge, 'that is the answer.'

1 Why does the judge think that the children have stolen the money?
_____ 2 marks

2 What does it mean when it says *'given what they could'*?
_____ 2 marks

3 Why does the judge describe Bobby as a *'special dog'*?
_____ 2 marks

4 Why can't the judge give Bobby a licence?
_____
_____ 2 marks

5 How does the judge sort out the problem?
_____
_____ 2 marks

Total: [ ]

STORYWORLDS BRIDGES: ASSESSMENT PCM 3 – STAGE 12
Skill: Literal and inferential comprehension.
Instructions: Read the story then answer the questions as fully as you can.